HAIKU

Other books by Nora D'Ecclesis...

Mastering Tranquility
Developing Powerful Stress Management Skills

Tranquil Seas
Applying Guided Visualization

Reiki Roundtable

The Retro Budget Prescription
Skillful Personal Planning

I'm So Busy!
Efficient Time Management

Lock Your Door
Passwords, PINS & Hackers

The Retro Budget Journal

HAIKU

NATURES MEDITATION

BY NORA D'ECCLESIS

Published by Renaissance Presentations, LLC
King of Prussia, PA
ISBN-13: 978-0692485798
ISBN-10: 0692485791
First Edition: July, 2015

Photographs courtesy of Danielle Dellacroce:
BlissfullyWhimsyPhotography.com

DEDICATION

TO "CHIO IN THE MORNING" TIM ACOSTA

Chio is a radio host in Philadelphia. His Philly show is fabulous and I still wake early to listen to his words of wisdom, keen wit and insight into human nature. Several years back we started a program of meditation and stress management and Chio listened to my suggestions with an attentiveness and fascination in my teachings. Chio implemented the techniques and over the years he developed a wonderful meditative program. I remember trying to get him to change the day we could meet and he always said politely "sorry Nora, Friday is not good". He is a strong quiet giant away from the microphone, a man's man with the gentleness and compassion of a Zen Bodhisattva. Much later in our friendship I learned he always worked and donated to the local soup kitchen on Fridays and for that I say, well done my friend doing service on your day off. It's ok for me to tell them Chio, you are a good guy, that type of man my mother always told me would give you the shirt off his back. Be well Tim.

Table of Contents

Introduction

Life is by its very nature impermanent. It is that impermanence that makes us rejoice at the sight of beauty in natural settings. The philosophy of Japanese Zen is consistent with haiku enthusiasts, making them a perfect match with this form of poetry. The elder haiku writers appreciated the impermanence of the scenes in nature and felt that moment would be gone in an instant making it even more beautiful.

Many early haiku poets were Buddhist from the Japanese group known as Zen, where haiku was an expressive art. Zen emphasizes staying in the present. The form of three lines of five, seven and five syllables make haiku poetry the short expression of nature and seasonal change. It permits the person reading to interpret the meaning.

Haiku does not require any special technique or equipment like most art. The simple tools of pen and paper enable anyone anywhere to be a poet. Haiku is three short little lines in a small poem that speaks volumes about how we think when viewing nature. We connect our true feelings of things in nature with a hint of the season and how we perceive it. Once touched by the words in the haiku poem our feelings flow in free association. Haiku is seeing beauty in nature and then expressing it in the written word describing how we feel about it.

History of Haiku

Matsuo Basho was born, Matsuo Chuemon Munefusa, in 1644 in Edo or modern Tokyo and was the world's greatest haiku writer. He was born into a Samurai family but elected to become a teacher in Edo and joined the intellectual world rather than the military. He wrote what was then called Hokku. Bosho took the pen name of Sobo, which is a sino-Japanese nickname for Munefusa, and was first published at age 20. He eventually left teaching and started a journey into the wilderness on what was called Edo Five Routes or 5 highways between Tokyo and Kyoto, which at the time was very dangerous. It was as if after facing his fears on these dangerous paths that he was finally happy. Basho practiced Zen meditation. His trips took him to Kyoto and Mt. Fuji and he was able to observe the seasons so his writing became less introspective and more about nature. He eventually returned back to his home area to teach but continued writing haiku. Basho occasionally entertained male muses but seemed to grow reclusive and preferred his huts alone. Finally in 1694 he became sick with a stomach issue which was his fatal illness. The similarities to Siddhartha or the historical Buddha are fascinating and of course Zen was a part of Basho's life so he did study the Buddhist teachings. Bosho's last poem:

Falling sick on a journey

my dream goes wondering

over a field of dried grass

By the 1800's the Shinto culture of Japan had deified Basho so everyone had to love him, but most did anyway.

The one exception to come along was Masaoka Tsunenori or his pen name, Shiki born September 17, 1867 and writing poetry by age 15. He was expelled from middle school due to his radical ideology and quit college. He was with the Japanese army as a correspondent during the Sino-Japanese War. His illness caused fatigue and fever and he soon realized his tuberculosis was getting worse. He returned home to write poetry after serving in the military. Shiki was very influenced by the western style of poetry writing. He felt poetry should be about things as they are in reality. He wrote in contemporary speech and placed haiku in the category of literature. The word HAIKU was first introduced to us by Shiki. He felt hokku should be used as the indication of the opening verse of renku. He was a prolific writer of haiku but unfortunately his tuberculosis got worse and he died young at age 34 on September 19, 1902. Shiki had two students, Kyoshi who felt haiku should contain poetry about nature and

Hekigodo the other student who felt it could be about any subject.

Taniguchi Yosa Buson (1716-1784)

Buson was a leading painter and haiku writer from Edo and Kyoto. His haiku was impressionistic but maintained haiku rules. TanTaigi and KuroyNgi Shoha helped Buson develop spontaneous style even though their styles were very different. Buson became the central figure of a haiku revival known as the return to Basho movement.

Busson's group built a Basho Hut for haiku and linked verse gatherings. Buson created many illustrated scrolls and screens including text of Oku which helped canonize Basho as a grand saint of poetry. Yosa married and had a child and lived to 68.

Kobayashi Issa (1762-1826)

6

Issa was a sensitive man and ordained as a Buddhist priest of the Pure Land tradition. Issa means, "cup of tea". He wrote of nature's imperfections in his haiku. Isaa faced many tragedies including the death of his mother at three and then the death of his wife and children. He was a prolific artist as well as a poet. "The Buddhism of the haiku contrasts with the Zen of the sketch"* *RH Blyth, *A History of Haiku Vol I* (Tokyo 1980) p.371

Issa is quoted in JD Salinger's 1961 novel <u>Franny and Zooey</u>

O snail
Climb Mount Fuji
But slowly, slowly!

These poetic giants were opening the gates of possibilities in both Japan and America.

Haiku Style

Haiku in three short lines is a small poem that speaks volumes about how we think while viewing nature. We connect our true feelings of things in nature with a hint of the season and how we perceive it. The poet is motivated by the words in the haiku poem and feelings flow in free association. Haiku is seeing beauty in nature and then expressing it in the written word how we feel about it. Haiku takes place in the present, a moment in time.

Traditional haiku has some key elements: Kigo, Kireji, Saikiki and Kiru.

Kigo is the traditional haiku reference to the season. The kigo alludes to the season for example spring might be young grass, cherry blossoms…. or frog peepers. Kigo are frequently in the metonyms or figures of speech that we use in place of the actual wording. It is the name of an association rather than its real name. An example would be Wall Street for financial services, Hollywood for the motion picture industry, the track for horse or dog racing and crown for the royal family, etc.

Kiru is a cutting in the poem and the most important part of haiku. It separates the juxtaposition in the haiku.

Kireji in traditional haiku always has a cutting word that divides the poem into sections with the purpose of each section helping to accent the understanding.

Many American haiku writers use a dash or ellipsis to substitute for kireji.

Saijiki is a reference pool from brainstorming a sort of dictionary for Kigo. It includes many trigger words from the seasons for use in the haiku.

The seasonal haikus contain many references: In Japan they are divided according to the dates each season begins and ends.

SAIJIKI EXAMPLES:

Spring- young love, pure, ethical, marriage, tranquil, serene, plow, herbs, silkworms, blossoms, azalea, buds, sprouts, nori, frogs

Summer- beach, sea, excess heat, sky blue, hot, south wind, fragrant breeze, evening downpour, thunder, drought, dripping waterfall, straw mats, rice planting, swimming, cutting grass, fireworks, airing, smog, cicada

Fall- loss, end of relationships, leaves changing, mysterious, autumn air, night chill, harvest moon, dew frost, mackerel clouds

Winter- snow, ice, no leaves, loss, NYE, short day, no leaves, fireplace, bonfire, hawk, wood burning stove, porridge, seven herbs, cold, freezing, windy

Styles for Writing Haiku

The most basic system to use when writing haiku is to ask questions and answer them in the poem. When writing haiku the writer simply answers the questions. The writer answers *what* the haiku is about, *where* it is taking place, which season is represented and perhaps even a *time period*. The writer can then organize the poem to obtain the desired effect.

Here is an example of the way Basho did it:

Blowing Stones

Along the road on Mount Asama

The autumn wind.

The *what* in this poem would be the blowing stones. The *where* would be along the road on Mount Asama. The *when* would be in the fall due to the use of the words "the autumn wind". The simplicity of this style does make it the perfect place to start as a student of haiku. Like any haiku, what matters is the impact of the content.

Juxtaposition is very common in many haikus. It involves taking separate images and showing a relationship between them. There are many types of relationships that can be shown between distinct images. The haiku can take the images and show a contrast depending on the desired realization or understanding.

Here is an example of Basho expressing a similarity between two distinctly different things:

Felling a tree

And seeing the cut end -

Tonight's moon.

Basho is expressing the similar look between the ring portion of a cut tree to the full moon.

Here is an example of contrast in a haiku written by Basho:

The winter sun —

On the horse's back

My frozen shadow.

In this haiku Basho expresses the contrast between the winter sun, which can give off slight relieving warmth, to the harshness of the cold winter. This also relates to how nothing in life is permanent. Even though it is winter there is slight warmth from the sun, however that sun may not last and the bitter cold will return.

Here is an example of an association haiku written by Basho:

This autumn —

Why am I growing old?

Bird disappearing among clouds.

In this haiku Basho is associating aging and losing his youth to the fall where things tend to die off and go dormant. The birds disappearing can be associated to his youth leaving him.

One exciting way to write haiku is by the suspense of what I call crescendo much like … "coming next on the news". This style is used at night when all the TV watcher is interested in is the weather report but the meteorologist slowly gives us small parts of the forecast saving the best for the last few minutes of the broadcast. Using this style the main subject of the haiku is gradually exposed throughout the poem. It is mystery being revealed. With each line the poem builds to inform us of the final subject matter. An example of the crescendo style written by Basho:

Autumn moonlight –

A worm digs silently

Into the chestnut.

The overall image is nothing more than a worm eating away at some chestnut, but it is the way Basho creates the scene in the reader's mind that makes this types of haiku so effective. Basho paints a scene of a full moon on an autumn night, then leads into the worm digging silently. Most readers would assume the worm would be eating dirt, but then Basho reveals that the worm is digging into a fine wood.

The key to writing unveiling haiku is to create a sense of mystery and that something is coming next. Treat the haiku like a strange puzzle. Start with a vague scene, provide a small detail, and then finish the puzzle with the final piece.

I like the general to the specific approach in haiku which involves starting with a broad scene and focusing down into a small point or element of the scene. The specific to the general involves the exact opposite starting with a single point or element of a scene and expanding outward to the entire broad scene.

Here is an example of the general to the specific technique written by Basho:

Spring rain

Leaking through the roof

Dripping from the wasps'
nest.

Basho starts very broad with the imagery of a spring rain shower. He then focuses in to the rain leaking through a roof. He focuses even further now to the rain water dripping from a wasps' nest. Basho went from a broad image all the way to a single element of the nest. This shows the beauty of nature from a broad scene all the way down to an intricate detail. Life exists on all scales large and small.

Here is an example of a specific to the general haiku written by Basho:

A crow

Has settled on a bare branch

Autumn evening.

Basho starts with a focused image of a crow. It is very simple and detailed. Basho then focuses out to the crow now sitting on a bare branch. He expands even further now to the image of an autumn evening. Basho started with the basic image of a crow and builds to an image of a vast autumn night scene where the reader envisions leaves fluttering in a cool fall breeze with a full moon.

There is a style of writing haiku that is imbedded in its very origins. Shiki liked this when he learned it from Basho and suggested that we write from a realistic perspective exactly what we were experiencing in our lives. How simple is that?

Here is an example of the basic realism style by Basho:

A snowy morning –

By myself

Chewing on dried salmon

This haiku accurately depicts a morning experience of Basho's. We have all had those mornings where we are gazing out the window munching on something with that same contented feeling of "ok let's start this day" and proceeded to do just that after we finished our bacon!

One of my personal favorite American haiku writers is Richard Wright. He used realism of activities in this haiku:

In the falling snow

A laughing boy holds out his palms

Until they are white.

How To Write Your First Haiku

➢   Go hiking in a beautiful natural setting.

➢   Take a pad and pencil and a smart phone for pictures if you have one.

➢   Stop near the stream and watch the snow melting and how it causes the water to rush faster. Photograph it or even better make a video. Take notes and how it makes you feel and what thoughts are entering your mind. Write how you feel and what you see at that moment.

➢ Log the sensory input.

    o Include:

       SMELLS

       SOUNDS

       EMOTIONS

       SIGHTS

       COLORS

➢ Write a list of key words coming into your mind. They might include, gloomy, sweltering, aroma, salty, taste buds

➢ Now you become the poet. Write two lines from the experience without form. Just write it.

➢ Return now to your desk to fine tune the poem with style and form. View everything again, the key words and the pictures.

➢ Write one more line that has nothing to do with the first two lines of your poem. Now, using your fingers count the syllables in the first two line omitting or adding as needed to bring the poem to standard haiku form. (I use my fingers)

- o 5

- o 7

- o 5

A syllable is a unit of organization for a sequence of speech sounds. They are the way we first teach phonics and reading. There are several types of syllables in English, closed (syllable with a short vowel) or open (ending with a long vowel sound) and complex with consonant and one vowel.

For our purposes let's look at how to better understand a syllable:

The word reading has two syllables: read - ing

As a middle school teacher years ago I taught my students to clap each syllable which made it fun.

Examples of syllables:

Cat
Sun set
Air plane
Ra di o
Book
Won der ful

Shintoism

Shinto, or Shintoism, is one of the oldest religions of Japan and uniquely Japanese. It teaches that Japan is the country of the Gods and people there are descendants. Shintoism is unique in that it is an action-centered religion with high importance placed on ritual practices that are carried out thoroughly to create a deep spiritual connection between the present and the ancients of the past. There are no specific guidelines or a "code of ethics" like many other religions contain as in "this is good, this is bad. Do this, do not do that". Shinto teaches important ethical principles but has no commandments.

The name Shinto is derived from the Chinese characters for Shen meaning "divine being" and Tao meaning "way". Therefore Shinto means "way of the spirits" or "way of the Gods". What also makes Shintoism unique is that it originated and is practiced strictly in Japan and Japan only. Shintoism is deeply rooted and values the traditions and history of Japan. What makes it nearly impossible to practice Shintoism elsewhere is the importance placed on shrines. Shrines hold a deep importance and are the backbone of the religion. There are between 80,000 and 100,000 Shinto shrines spread throughout Japan.

Shintoism has no specific God. There is no founder of the religion. There is not a specific scripture such as the Bible for Christians or Qur'an for Islam. Many experts cannot even agree on the time period that Shinto may have begun. At the heart of Shinto is the devotion to spiritual beings and powers which are referred to as *kami* which exist in nature. Shintoism is very nature driven. *Kami* can be defined in English as "spirit", "spiritual essence", or "God". The divine or sacred essence can manifest in many forms such as a tree, rock, body of water, animal, a place, or even a person. Those practicing Shinto believe that people and kami exist in the same world and are interconnected. A focus of Shinto is to honor one's family *kami* and ancestors.

The religion of Shintoism has been broken down into categories. There are many different sects and schools but most scholars can agree on the three main categories of Shinto, the first being Shrine Shinto. This category focuses strongly in worshiping local shrines kept in the home and also taking part in events held at local shrines around one's living area. Another type of Shinto is Folk Shinto. The focus of this category is the numerous folk beliefs in spirits and gods although many of the beliefs seem to be uneven and disjointed. Followers of Folk Shinto tend to believe in spirit possession and healing from the source of a shaman. The beliefs and practices of Folk Shinto come from local ancient traditions which are why the beliefs are so fragmented. However, some practices are influenced by

Buddhism, Taoism or Confucianism. The third category is Sect Shinto. Sect Shinto was created in the 1890s with the purpose to separate government owned shrines from local organized religious communities. The difference between Shrine Shinto and Sect Shinto is that the followers of Sect Shinto believe that through the power of their consciousness they can identify a founder of Shinto, a set of teachings, and sacred scriptures.

Again, no matter what category of Shinto a person falls under there is still a heavy importance placed on shrines. Shrines are where a person worships a *kami* or spirit. Public shrines are sacred places that act as an access point to a *kami*. People visit them to pray or make offerings of food. Shrines can be man-made or pure natural places such as a tree, waterfall, or a mountain. Shrines that are natural are referred to as *mori*.

Many public shrines are elaborate structures whose architecture will fit the period in which the shrine was built with appropriate traditional Japanese design. At the entrance to these shrines is a Japanese gate called a *tori*. The *tori* is made of two uprights and two crossbars. The purpose of the *tori* is to show a division between the common world and a sacred area. At most shrines there will only be one way of access, but some shrines will have two ways of access and both paths will have a *tori*. Although all *tori* contain two uprights and two crossbars there are around twenty styles based on the kami being worshiped and the lineage of the local area and shrine. Also at these public shrines it is common to see other barriers that act as separations from the common world and the sacred spiritual world and shrine grounds. There are clear barriers like fences, ropes, gated paths, and statues of protection.

The practice of visiting a shrine is called *Omairi*. It is important to note that one does not have to identify as Shinto in order to visit a shrine.

There are steps to take when visiting a shrine and the steps can vary depending on the shrine, season, holiday, or overall reason for the visit depending on what a person is praying or making an offering for. At any entrance to the shrine one should bow respectfully before passing through the *tori*. Typically there is a hand washing basin provided near the shrine. There is a specific way in which to cleanse one's hands. Hold the ladle in the right hand and scoop up water and pour it onto the left hand. Then transfer the ladle to the left hand and pour water onto the right hand. Place the ladle in the right hand again, make a cup with the left hand, and pour water into the left hand. Take the water from the left hand and sip it into the mouth. Quietly swish the water around in the mouth then spit the water back into the cupped left hand. After, grab the ladle handle with both hands and turn it vertically so the remaining water washes over the handle. Place the ladle where it was found.

After a proper hand cleansing is completed one can approach the shrine. Some shrines may have a bell and this would be the appropriate time to ring the bell. Other shrines may have a donation box to deposit a donation in before ringing the bell. It is appropriate and expected to leave a donation based on the level or impact of one's prayer. After donating or ringing the bell, or both, bow twice, clap twice holding the second clap. One should hold their hands together in front of the heart for a closing bow after a prayer is made.

One should be as quiet as possible while on the sacred grounds and at the shrine. No shoes should be worn in any buildings on the sacred grounds. One must be respectful and sincere to all staff and others visiting the shrine. Pay attention to areas where people are not permitted to go on the shrine grounds.

The spirituality of Shinto teaches the unity of nature:

- o Tradition and the family
- o Love of nature
- o Physical cleanliness
- o Worship ancestral spirits.

History of Siddhartha

It is not necessary to know anything about Buddhism to write haiku but it certainly is interesting, educational and helps to appreciate the philosophy of the early haiku writers.

Who was this man we call Buddha and how did he formulate his ideas and philosophy known as the Noble Path?

Many years ago...approximately 2700 years past....

Queen Maha Maya and King Suddhodana owned the municipality of Kapilavastu in an area of India now known as Nepal. Late in life the queen realized she was pregnant and with great joy informed her husband.

Maya wanted to go back to her parents because her baby was almost due. Since it was the custom in India for a wife to have her baby in her father's house, the king agreed. So, the King made the arrangements for his queen to travel in royal style.

On the way to the Koliya country, the great procession passed a garden called Lumbini Park. This garden was near the kingdom called Nepal, at the foot of the Himalayan Mountains. It was very warm and Queen Maya decided to go wading into a lake. Shortly after that she went into labor and holding the branches of a tree she gave birth to son who would be named. Siddhartha Gotama.

The birth took place on a full moon which is now celebrated as Vesak, the festival of the triple event of Buddha's birth, enlightenment and death, in the year 623 B.C.E. This date is still in question and subject *to much debate. The times of Gautama's birth and death are uncertain: most historians in the early 20th century dated his lifetime as circa 563 BCE to 483 BCE but more recent opinion dates his death to between 486 and 483 BCE or, according to some, between 411 and 400 BCE- However, at a symposium on this question held in 1988, the majority of those who presented definite opinions gave dates within 20 years either side of 400 BCE for the Buddha's death. These alternative chronologies, however, have not yet been accepted by all other historians.* *

*Hans Wolfgang Schumann (2003). The Historical Buddha: The Times, Life, and Teachings of the Founder of Buddhism, p. xv. Motilal Banarsidass Publ. ISBN 8120818172

After the birth of her baby son, Queen Maha Maya immediately returned to Kapilavastu to present the King his son. The infant was given the name Siddhartha in Pāli: Siddhartha, meaning "he who achieves his aim". Seven days after her return home Queen Maya died. Siddhartha was born in a royal Hindu family and many helped care for him. He was brought up by his mother's younger sister, Maha Pajapati.

The king was devastated and called for advice from his advisors to help him understand why the joyful birth of his son caused the death of his wife. The king also wanted to know what type of life his new child would have and how he should raise him so he called for Asita a hermit who was ascetic and had great psychic powers. Asita predicted that the Prince Siddhartha of Kapilavastu would either become a great king, called a chakravartin or become a spiritual leader and Buddha.

The king did everything he could think of to be certain his son Prince Siddhartha would grow up prepared for a life following in his own footsteps and become a king of the municipality. The prince was taught archery and math and fighting skills as a young child but always showed signs of compassion and refused to hunt.

When he reached the age of 16, the king arranged the prince's marriage to a cousin of the same age named Yasodhara. It is said he did so because the future Buddha was so kind and gentle and the uncles suggested he needed a wife to make him more "manly". The young prince and princess enjoyed a charmed life so important to the future Buddha's story. It is during this time that Siddhartha's philosophy of life was formed. He lived in total luxury.

Of his luxurious life as a prince he states:

"I was delicate, excessively delicate. In my father's dwelling three lotus ponds were made purposely for me. Blue Lotuses bloomed in one, red in another, and white in the third. I used no sandwood that was not kasi. My turban, tunic, dress and cloak were all kasi. Night and day a white parasol was held over me so that I might not be touched by heat or cold, dust leaves or dew."

"There were three palaces built for me- one for the cold season, one for the hot season, one for the rainy season. During the four rainy months, I lived in the palace for the rainy season, entertained by female musicians, without coming down from the palace. Just as in the houses of others, food from the husks of rice together with sour gruel is given to the slaves and workmen, even so, in my father's dwelling, food with rice and

*meat was given to the slaves and workmen". ***

*"A Manual of Buddhism", Narada, 1992, Kuala Lumpur, Malaysia

We begin to see a pattern of the future Buddha growing bored with the ostentatious lifestyle of his father. However, his father was a great King who treated all humans well in a time when that was not the norm. Prince Siddhartha's starts to question the meaning of life and what lies beyond the walls of Kapilavastu at about the same time Yaśodhara got pregnant after all those years.

According to the history, she gave birth to a son, named Rahula who was named by his father. It is interesting to note the meaning of the name Rahula - a soft fetter or chain.

Siddhartha is said to have spent twenty-nine years as a prince in Kapilavastu. Although his father ensured that Siddhartha was provided with everything he could want or need, Buddhist scriptures say that the future Buddha felt that materialism was not what gave his life meaning. So the prince requested that his father permit him to enter the city on the other side of the wall. The prince went on a journey and saw old age for the first time.

When the prince saw the old man, he didn't know what was wrong with this man. It was the first time in his life that he had seen an old person.

The next sighting was of a man crying out in pain in a scream. This made the prince very sad. Channa who was Siddhartha's friend tried to explain that everyone in this world will eventually get sick, old and die. Buddha asks, 'Why does a man lie there so still, allowing people to burn him? It's as if he does not know anything.' Channa explained the man was dead. Channa explained that the happy men walking around smiling were monks seeking spiritual truths. The Buddha thought that perhaps he would like being a monk.

The prince felt very happy now and decided to become a monk. He walked until he was tired, then sat under a tree to think some more. As he was sitting under the cool shady tree, news came that his wife had given birth to a fine baby boy. Siddhartha felt the baby to be an impediment, Rahula has been born and he felt him to be an obstacle to leaving.

Siddhartha was determined to leave anyway so Channa prepared his horse and Siddhartha went to see his newborn son for the first time. His wife was sleeping with the baby beside her. The prince decided to go without waking them to finish what he was looking for and he felt that at some point he would return. Prince Siddhartha left his father's estate, took off his robes and cut his hair to two fingers breath. He became known as ascetic Gautama. He walked all over Northern

Indian for almost six years fasting and seeking enlightenment.

Siddhartha decided to sit under a banyan tree to meditate, he was very weak. A young woman named Sujata saw him and offered sweet thick milk rice in a golden bowl. When he finished he took the golden bowl and threw it in the river. He felt if this bowl floated upstream he would give up the path of asceticism. The golden bowl went upstream keeping in the middle of the river. He decided at that moment to sit and meditate until he was enlightened. After he sat for days and faced his demons, Buddha achieved enlightenment.

The first teaching ever given by the Buddha was to five student monks in a deer park. The Buddha spoke of the Four Noble Truths he had discovered while struggling for enlightenment, these are the central teachings of Buddhism.

"Learn The Rules & Then Forget Them"

Haiku from Japan to America...

In 1913 Ezra Pound published the first haiku written in English. It came from an experience he had in a Paris subway. The entire haiku was only 14 words that in my opinion exemplifies the existential notion that life is of the nature of impermanence. The poem is called *"In a Station of the Metro"*. Check it out and know that American haiku started with him. It is also interesting to make note of why some of Basho's poems quoted in this book do not appear to conform to the 5-7-5 suggested format.

Japanese haiku counts sounds not syllables. The work haiku has two syllables in English but in Japanese it has three sounds. The word Tokyo has three syllables toe-key-oh in English but in

Japanese toe-oh-kyo-oh has four sounds and basically four syllables.

In *"The Poetics of Japanese Verse"*, by Koji Sakamoto it is taught the word sign has one syllable but in Japanese three sounds sig-ya-n. In both Japanese and English we all agree that the word sushi has two sounds and two syllables which makes me very happy because it is my favorite food and I enjoy including the word sushi in my poetry. The point of haiku is to convey feelings.

Basho said, "Learn the rules and then forget them". Sage advice. Be well.

Haiku by D'Ecclesis

Explosion of life

Cherry Blossoms awaken

Tastebuds come alive

d'ecclesis

A strand of birch trees

Deciduous hardwood gift

Wood makes nice guitar

d'ecclesis

Rapids picking up
Around the bend mystery
To bail out or stay

d'ecclesis

Rocks rounded by time

Riverbed ever changing

The pike stalks its prey

d'ecclesis

A money tree plant

Pachira aquatica

Growth spurt abundance!

d'ecclesis

Ancient oaks stand guard

The forgotten woods timeless

Gone forest fire

d'ecclesis

Mt Etna rumbles

A surge of molten lava

Ancient beast wakes up

d'ecclesis

Equanimity—
Grounded from adversity
Nimbus clouds appear

d'ecclesis

All cares disappear
Takeoff exhilarating
  Elevates my thoughts

       d'ecclesis

At the crack of dawn

The Hyacinth's aroma

The runner goes by

d'ecclesis

The Pesse canoe

Fingers in cool lake water

Serene glide slow stream

d'ecclesis

Watching the white tail
The deer steps elegantly
Chunks of ice float by

d'ecclesis

West to Pacific

Continental divide streams

East to Atlantic

d'ecclesis

Northern lights in spring

Kaleidoscope of color

Reykjavik Iceland

d'ecclesis

Pink cherry blossoms

Magnolia tree in blossom

Eating mulberries

d'ecclesis

Autumn afternoons
A multitude of colors—
Brown bears lumber by

d'ecclesis

Roasting marshmallows

On the open fire pit

Don't need chocolate

d'ecclesis

Winter sun, blue sky
Months of ice and snow ahead
Dusk on dark mountain

d'ecclesis

Mountains of wet snow

The blizzard pounds the corn fields

Howling wind scares dog

d'ecclesis

Black ravens scavenge
Autumn leaves piled high outside
Halloween candy!

d'ecclesis

The spring equinox
Climbs up the magnolia tree
Bug bites pulling weeds

d'ecclesis

White cap waves crashing
Gorgeous cumulus clouds
Hermit crab left shell

d'ecclesis

Nor'easter brings ice—
Snow like a Russian novel
A single finch chirps

d'ecclesis

Shoden starts the class
Okuden healing insight
Shinpiden master

d'ecclesis

A Place To
Start Writing...

5

7

5

5 _____

7 _____

5 _____

5

7

5

5

_____

7

_____

5

_____

_____
5

_____
7

_____
5

5 _____

7 _____

5 _____

5

7

5

5

7

5

_____

5

_____

7

_____

5

5

7

5

About The Author

Amazon Bestselling Author Nora D'Ecclesis is an American author who writes non-fiction books to help mitigate stress. She is a graduate of Kean University, with a degree in education, graduate degree in administration and post-graduate degree including certification as a learning specialist.

Nora D'Ecclesis has a long history of presenting events focused on wellness and stress reduction techniques. She enjoys kayaking, hiking and archery. Nora lives with her family and wonderful dogs in a suburb of Philadelphia, Pennsylvania.

For more information, visit **noradecclesis.com**

53357442R00056

Made in the USA
Lexington, KY
01 July 2016